GOD MOMENTS
FOR DARK DAYS

40 meditations to lift your spirits

Jennifer Rees Larcombe

MONARCH
BOOKS

Oxford, UK, and Grand Rapids, USA

Published by Monarch Books
an imprint of
Lion Hudson plc
Wilkinson House, Jordan Hill Road,
Oxford OX2 8DR, England
Email: monarch@lionhudson.com
www.lionhudson.com/monarch

ISBN 978 0 85721 694 6

First edition 2016

Acknowledgments
See page 93

A catalogue record for this book is available from the British Library

Printed and bound in Poland, December 2015, LH44

For my daughter, Sarah

Contents

1	One Day at a Time	9
2	Collapse	10
3	Fireball	13
4	Worst Fear	16
5	Door of Hope	18
6	The Bird's Nest	20
7	Standing Still	21
8	The "Yes" in My Heart	24
9	Words That Mess with Our Heads	28
10	Healing Grace for Others	30
11	The Shetland Shawl	32
12	Spring Will Come Again	34
13	Stolen Joy	36
14	Loved Forever	38
15	Lace Handkerchief	40
16	VDPs	42
17	Giving Up Our Right	46
18	Playing Ball	48
19	Just Float	49
20	Flickering Flame	51
21	Lost in the Maze	52

22	Oranges	55
23	The Wise Old Monk	58
24	Limitless Supply	60
25	The Jewel Box	63
26	Prisoners	65
27	Where Do We Place Our Hope?	67
28	Flood Tide	68
29	The Child Inside	70
30	Forgotten Your Password?	71
31	Held	73
32	Faith in His Faithfulness	74
33	Stuck in the Mud	76
34	Peace in Action	80
35	Scars	82
36	Shadows	83
37	Forgive and Forget	84
38	The King's Speech	85
39	Choose Life	87
40	Snowdrops	88

1
One Day at a Time

Have you ever felt you didn't have enough strength to keep going any longer? The situation you are in is just *too* draining and exhausting. Maybe the Lord wants you to cling onto this promise; "As your *days*, so shall your strength be" (Deuteronomy 33:25 NKJV). He wants you to take this situation "one day at a time" and He is promising to give you all the strength you are going to need for that one day.

> *But I trust in You, Lord; I say, "You are my God."*
> *My times are in Your hands.*
>
> Psalm 31:14–15

Lord, I sometimes feel I can't face one more hour, let alone a whole day! So help me trust You for an hourly dose of strength instead.

2
Collapse

"Why God?" we sometimes shout when our lives explode, but when you're as old as I am you can look back and see that it was during the bad times that you discovered the depth of God's tenderness – as well as His ability to rebuild broken lives. In His first sermon Jesus used the following words to introduce Himself to us.

> "The Spirit of the Sovereign Lord is on me... He has sent me to bind up the broken-hearted... to bestow on them a crown of beauty instead of ashes... They will rebuild the ancient ruins and restore the places long devastated; they will renew the ruined cities that have been devastated..."
>
> Isaiah 61:1, 3, 4

GOD MOMENTS FOR DARK DAYS

It was to people like us who say, "Why God?" that Jesus came to bring hope.

Lord, I feel I'm stranded in the ruins of all my dreams, hopes, and plans. So many things have changed or been lost that it feels like I have no points of reference left. Help me to grasp the truth that You are "the same yesterday, today and forever" (Hebrews 13:8). You are my one safe, unchanging benchmark.

3
Fireball

Yesterday I was sitting in my prayer corner but I was too angry to pray. I felt there was a huge fireball of rage inside me which had become a wall between me and God. I tried to calm myself

down, repeat soothing verses and thank Him for everything I could think of, but still the fire blocked Him out. Finally, in desperation, I asked Him to come round to my side of the fire, fully expecting that He would tell me to do some serious forgiving! Still nothing, so I went out and watered my plants.

Then, suddenly I realized that my anger had its root in fear not resentment – fear of my own inadequacy and failure in a particular situation in which I felt stuck. As I sensed the Lord saying, "We both know you can't cope with what's happened, so why don't you just accept your inability as a fact, ask Me into the centre of the mess and let Me take responsibility." The fear and anger were replaced by a wonderful sense of relief!

> *My grace is enough; it's all you need. My strength comes into its own in your weakness.*
>
> 2 Corinthians 12:9, THE MESSAGE

> *Lord, help me to stop focusing so much on my own inadequacy and embrace Your total adequacy instead!*

4
Worst Fear

What is your very worst fear? For many of us it's known as FOMO – Fear Of Missing Out – which means not being special to anyone: forgotten, ignored, useless. The good news is that God says we never have to experience FOMO when we belong to Him.

Just look at "You are precious in My sight and honoured and… I love you" (Isaiah 43:4 AMP) and "Even the very hairs of your head are all numbered" (Matthew 10:30). And He *never* stops thinking about us.

> *The eyes of the Lord range throughout the*
> *earth to strengthen those whose hearts are fully*
> *committed to him.*

2 Chronicles 16:9

No more FOMO for me!

Lord, all my life I've been hungry for love and approval; help me to realize that I'll never be fully satisfied while I look for them from other people. You are the source of everything I need.

5
Door of Hope

Have you ever had the feeling that your whole life has exploded and you are buried under the rubble and debris of everything you once valued?

The people who were listening to Hosea preach would have known he was describing this feeling when he mentioned the Valley of Achor. A whole family were once killed and buried there together. Hosea was actually saying that even in the most ghastly place of trouble God has placed "a door of hope and expectation" (Hosea 2:15, AMP).

Jesus said He was the Door, so *our* hope for rescue and restoration lies in Him. He has never yet ignored a cry for help from someone buried in the darkness and I'm convinced He never will.

> *"I am the Door; anyone who enters in through Me will be saved. I came that they may have and enjoy life, and have it in abundance (to the full, till it overflows)."*
>
> John 10:9, AMP

Jesus, Door of Hope, I'm groping my way towards You, even though it is too dark to see if You are there at all. By faith alone I am going to push on that door until it opens and I can walk back into the light.

6
The Bird's Nest

There is a bird's nest wedged between the bare branches of a tree in my garden. Last summer it was hidden by pretty leaves; and now winter has left it exposed to terrible gales and lashing rain – yet it's survived them all! Maybe you feel all your comfortable, protective "leaves" have been lost, leaving you battered by storms? God wants you to know that He is so proud of your faith in Him, which has held you in place, like the bird's nest.

> *"Great is the Lord, who delights in blessing his servant with peace!"*
>
> Psalm 35:27, NLT

Thank You, Lord, for caring for me and watching me so lovingly. Sometimes I feel so alone up here in these storms. Other people just don't understand how it feels. Please help me respond with more grace to their unwanted advice and tactless comments!

7
Standing Still

"Let all that I am wait quietly before God, for my hope is in him" (Psalm 62:5, NLT).

Those words were written by a soldier in a war zone! They are for anyone whose life feels like that right now, with difficult things hitting you from all sides. The last thing you feel like doing is "waiting quietly". Instinctively you want to do something, organize the chaos, find a way out! David just stood still and waited until God showed him what to do next. "Let all that I am wait quietly…" that meant deliberately stilling his body, his mind, and his emotions while he allowed God to take control of the situation.

Could you dare to do that too?

"Be still, and know that I am God."

Psalm 46:10

Lord, I don't think I can learn to be deeply still and at peace until I am much better at appreciating what You mean by saying, "I AM GOD." Please increase my capacity to know just how powerful, how loving, how holy and how present You actually are!

8
The "Yes" in My Heart

Have you ever chosen a particular path through life because, at the time, you were convinced it was the one God wanted you to take? Then later, when the road became rough and steep did you ever wonder if you made the right decision? When I felt like that I kept hearing this little song on the radio: "I never promised you a rose garden". Through it Jesus reminded me that He never promised us an easy time on earth, because this life is only a prelude to our real life, which will begin when we step into eternity. What Jesus longs to see is the "yes" in our hearts as we respond to Him.

I have made up my mind. Until the darkness disappears and the dawn has fully come, in spite of shadows and fears – I will go to the mountain-top with you. I will climb with you the mountain of suffering love and the hill of burning incense (Song of Songs 4:6, Passion Translation).

Jesus said, "Peace, be still!" And the wind ceased and there was a great calm.

Mark 4:39, NKJV

9

Words That Mess with Our Heads

I was six years old, wearing my new coat and in London for a special treat. Our first stop was Trafalgar Square where a pigeon landed on my head and pooed massively all over my carefully plaited hair and new dress. No amount of hankie rubbing could make me feel anything but revolting until I finally got into a bath that night. Words can be dumped on us as easily as bird poo, and they can mess up the way we feel about ourselves for the rest of our lives. "You never get anything right! You're fat… unattractive… don't fit in here… useless… clumsy…" I believe that the power of Jesus can wash people clean from the harmful effects of those words, as easily as if they had been bird poo!

> *You will be called by a new name that the mouth of the Lord will bestow.*

Isaiah 62:2

Lord, I've grown up thinking that the destructive things people said to me or thought about me are actually true. I've built my self-image based on their inaccurate opinions. Please change the way I think about myself until it fits in with Your opinion of me, which You express so many times in the Bible.

10
Healing Grace for Others

Isn't it odd how you can meet someone and *just know* they understand what you are going through, and exactly how you feel – simply because they've been there too! So they absolutely never trot out irritating little platitudes or harass you with unasked-for advice. I used to have this quote by Amy Carmichael on my fridge: "Don't you think that some of us must know the trials of misty weather if we are to be enabled to understand when others are in the mist?"

> *Praise be to… the Father of compassion and the God of all comfort, who comforts us in all our troubles, so that we can comfort those in any trouble with the comfort we ourselves receive from God.*

2 Corinthians 1:3, 4

Lord, this situation that I'm going through feels such a waste – so destructive. But please would You use it one day to help somebody else?

11
The Shetland Shawl

When my first baby was born someone who lives on the Shetland Isles sent me a beautiful hand-knitted shawl. Sarah loved having it tucked round her as she drifted off to sleep. Even when she was five or six she still wanted its cosy warmth whenever she felt miserable.

After a very difficult week, I found a message in my inbox from a friend; she told me about a picture she "saw" of a Shetland shawl, which she felt the Lord had knitted Himself especially for me. She felt He wanted to wrap it round me as He sang over me.

> *The Lord your God in your midst, The Mighty One, will save; He will rejoice over you with gladness, He will quiet you with His love, He will rejoice over you with singing.*

Zephaniah 3:17, NKJV

Jesus, you told us that the best way to thrive
in Your Kingdom is to become like a little child
(Matthew 18:3). As I've got older, it seems
more difficult to receive comfort and kindness
– I feel I ought to be giving it to others
instead. Help me to accept Your cosseting
love, because there are times when I need it
so badly!

12
Spring Will Come Again

Last spring the blossom on my apple tree was better than ever before, so I looked forward to a wonderful crop of apples. However, during the summer I fractured my pelvis and wasn't able to climb my ladder to pick the apples as they ripened. I felt so sad when I saw them shrivelling on their branches or rotting on the ground.

Sometimes our lives are like my apple tree; at one stage so full of promise and potential, which gradually seems to become wasted and worthless. I think the Lord is saying to anyone who feels like that, "With Me there is always another blossom time, followed by a satisfying harvest. It is never too late to start again with Me. Your life is far too precious to Me to be wasted."

> *"For I know the plans I have for you… plans to prosper you… plans to give you hope and a future."*
>
> Jeremiah 29:11

Lord, please help me to accept Your wonderful promise to me.

13
Stolen Joy

Some people seem to be able to crush all the joy out of us – perhaps by their constant bad moods or uncontrollable bouts of anger. Actually it is impossible for anybody to rob us of joy because it is a supernatural gift, given to us by Jesus Himself. "I have told you this so that my joy may be in you and that your joy may be complete" (John 15:11). People can definitely rob us of happiness, which depends on outward circumstance, but joy is something so deep inside us that only we have the power to let it go. We can do this by reacting to this difficult person with resentment or suppressed rage, but if we choose to hold onto Jesus tightly and act and react as He would, then His joy will remain.

The joy of the Lord is your strength.

Nehemiah 8:10

Restore unto me the joy of your salvation
and grant me a willing spirit to sustain me.
(Psalm 51:12)

14
Loved Forever

The only man I ever loved, and married, eventually ran out of love for me – and found someone else. I was devastated, but discovering this verse changed everything. "The Lord said… 'I have loved you with an everlasting love; therefore with loving-kindness have I drawn you *and* continued my faithfulness to you'" (Jeremiah 31:3, AMP). Once you realize you're permanently loved and to such a depth nothing else matters!

> *Lord, please forgive me for the times in my*
> *life when I have doubted Your love for me,*
> *because You allowed such painful things to*
> *happen to me. Now, from the distance of time,*
> *I can see that You really did make all those*
> *hard things work together for good, just as You*
> *promised You would. (Romans 8:28)*

15
Lace Handkerchief

Isn't it hard when you feel utterly useless and inadequate in the situation that faces you – like offering someone with a bad cold a delicate lace handkerchief! I think the Lord is saying to me, and perhaps to you, "Stop trying to help other people in your own strength; I care about them infinitely more than you ever could, I even collect their tears in a bottle. Just keep on allowing all My love and compassion for them to flow through you."

> *You keep track of all my sorrows. You have collected all my tears in your bottle. You have recorded each one in your book.*

Psalm 56:8, NLT

*When my friends are suffering I never know
what to say or do. Lord, please would You
always give me Your wisdom for each one
individually? Show me if I should call round or
stay away; be sympathetic or bracing; try to
distract them or simply cry with them. Lord,
please let me share Your empathy.*

16
VDPs

Most of us have at least one VDP (Very Difficult Person) in our lives. Here's a good way of protecting ourselves from them. Often it is the sight of their fierce, angry face that feels so demoralizing but not looking at them makes them even more furious. I've found that picturing myself putting the cross of Jesus between me and my VDP really helps because then all their accusations and verbal abuse hits the cross first and Jesus absorbs all the pain.

> *The insults of those who insult you have fallen on me.*
>
> Romans 15:3

Lord, I'm afraid that next time I'm being hit by all that verbal abuse I'll forget You have promised to protect me. I am sure You will, but please do remind me!

Does my strength come from mountains?
No, my strength comes from God, who
made heaven, and earth, and mountains.
He won't let you stumble, … God won't
fall asleep.

Psalm 121:1–3, *THE MESSAGE*

17
Giving Up Our Right...

Forgiving isn't fashionable these days. After some terrible road accident or terrorist attack, survivors say proudly, "Well I'll definitely never forgive!" Perhaps they feel it is weakness to let someone "get away with it"? Followers of Jesus have to swim against the tide over this, because forgiving is something He definitely told us to do. "You can't get forgiveness from God… without also forgiving others" (Matthew 6:14, THE MESSAGE).

Because Christians find forgiveness as difficult as anyone else, we sometimes wriggle out of it by telling ourselves that we have to wait until the other person says sorry first. For us that is "out" too: Jesus forgave the soldiers who hammered His hands to the cross without any apology. Forgiveness actually means giving up our right to hear the other person *ever* say sorry. Fortunately Jesus never tells us to do anything He isn't prepared to help us to do!

If you forgive those who sin against you, your heavenly Father will forgive you. But if you refuse to forgive others, your Father will not forgive your sins.

Matthew 6:14–15, NLT

Lord, help me to remember that "Forgiveness is unlocking the door to set someone free – and realizing [I was] the prisoner." (Max Lucado)

18
Playing Ball

Did you know we can play ball with God? When I'm hit by a difficult emotion such as worry, resentment, or regret I can easily let it grow in my heart until it becomes destructive. So, instead I imagine myself rolling the feeling into a ball and throwing it up to God. He catches it and throws me down another ball in exchange. This ball is made up of the opposite emotion, perhaps peace, love, or forgiveness. I catch it and think of myself pulling it inside my heart.

> *Give all your worries and cares to God, for he cares about you.*
>
> 1 Peter 5:7, NLT

Lord, sometimes I feel I am better at giving You my difficult emotions, than receiving back from You their antidote. Show me how to find the perfect balance between "give" and "take".

19
Just Float

I remember once, during a time of confusion and change, feeling utterly exhausted by making endless fruitless plans, listening to conflicting advice and trying to hold everyone else together. One morning I felt there was no more fight left in me.

Then through the door came a card from an old friend. "Stop struggling to swim against this high tide, turn over and just let your spirit float in the ocean of God's love for a while. He'll wake you up and tell you when He wants you to take action."

The Lord will fight for you; you need only to be still.

Exodus 14:14

Lord I don't feel I even have enough energy to pray right now. Help me to rest on an air bed made from the prayers of my friends.

20
Flickering Flame

I love it that Jesus "will not crush the weakest reed or put out a flickering candle" (Matthew 12:20 NLT). Sometimes I feel my candle flame of spiritual energy and enthusiasm is burning very low and flickering dangerously. I love the way He just shields me with His hands until my flame burns steady  again; yet I never realize His hands are there at the time.

> *But you, Lord, are a shield around me, my glory,*
> *the One who lifts my head high.*
>
> Psalm 3:3

Lord Your patience astounds me!

21
Lost in the Maze

I took two of my grandchildren for a day out to Hever Castle, but the treat was ruined when we got lost in the maze. We would start off down a promising-looking path, only to meet with yet another dead end. The frustration was maddening, but the worst part was the sense that nobody else knew where we were. It was only the loud wailing of the children that eventually brought someone to our rescue. Life can feel like that maze too sometimes: full of disappointing dead ends, which seem unimportant to everyone else.

If you feel you are in a maze right now, I think the Lord is saying, "Trust Me just a little bit longer. I died the most painful death possible to win you, so how could I possibly abandon you now? You will find the right path, if you just keep trusting Me."

"I will lead the blind by ways they have not known, along unfamiliar paths I will guide them... I will not forsake them."

Isaiah 42:16

Thank You, Lord, that you see my maze from above, so it isn't confusing to You like it is to me. Thank You that You never abandon me to find my own way through life!

22
Oranges

Have you ever felt squeezed dry by other peoples' constant demands? Perhaps you feel your life is all about "give" and not enough "take"? I remember feeling exactly like that when I was caring for a house full of teenagers and an elderly mother-in-law. I was grumbling to the Lord one day when I felt He showed me a picture of an orange.

As I asked Him what it meant I realized that an orange is only useful when it has been peeled open and squeezed! It is then that it can share its sweetness and nourishing juice. If it keeps all that juice inside – it eventually rots. As I faced the piles of washing up that night I realized that it was a bit like Jesus allowing His life to be broken and poured out for others.

I am poured out like water... My heart has turned to wax; it has melted away within me.

Psalm 22:14

Jesus, I don't want to be squeezed, but I do want to be used by You. So please give me the courage to lie quietly in Your hands and the faith to be sure that You only ever want the best for me.

23
The Wise Old Monk

One of the people I most want to meet in heaven is a seventeenth-century monk called Brother Lawrence. He never learned to read or write and, because he couldn't sing the Latin chants, he was sent to work in the monastery kitchen. That made him sad because all he'd ever wanted to do was worship God. Gradually Lawrence realized that every single unimportant little job he did during his busy days of scrubbing pots and sweeping floors could actually be given to God as an act of worship. So he trained himself to remember that Jesus was standing beside him constantly, enjoying everything he was doing.

> *Whatever your hand finds to do, do it with all your might.*
>
> Ecclesiastes 9:10

Lord my anxiety levels are smashing through the roof this morning. I have so much to do, sort, and organize today that I simply don't

know where to begin! But this is what I feel You are saying to me:

"You can only effectively do one job at a time. So do the one you're doing now for ME. By the end of the day you'll have spent a whole day in worship. And I'll make sure you get through your Job List!"

24
Limitless Supply

I will never forget the day when I met Emmy. It was soon after she lost her sight, yet her face was so full of strength and peace that I asked for her secret. "When I was a child," she told me, "we lived next to an airport. All I could see from my bedroom window was a vast hangar – I used to think it must be the biggest building in the world!

"Money was very tight in our household yet my dad never worried. He would point at the aeroplane hangar and say, 'Our God has a treasure house, far larger than that, and it's full of everything we'll ever need. All we have to do is open the hangar door by asking for the Lord's help, and He'll push out exactly what we need.' I used to say: 'But supposing we empty it one day?' How he laughed. 'As we take the treasure out of the front door, so He pushes more in through the back door – so the building stays full all the time!' For years I thought that was literally true until

I grew old enough to realize that, in the spiritual realm, it *is* true. As the old hymn says, 'All I have needed thy hand hath provided, great is thy faithfulness, Lord, unto me.'"

> *My God will liberally supply (fill to the full) your every need according to His riches in glory in Christ Jesus.*
>
> Philippians 4:19 AMP

Thank You, Lord, that I can never come to the end of my "fair share" of Your blessings! Please help me to take this promise so deeply into my heart and mind that I can live constantly in Your peace.

25
The Jewel Box

I used to love it when my granny showed me her jewels. Each one was so precious to her because it carried a memory of a person or special occasion. Now some of them live in my jewellery box, to be shown to my grandchildren. God says He has a collection of precious jewels too, which delight Him. You're part of that collection and so am I, no matter how worthless and rubbishy we may feel.

They shall be Mine, says the Lord of hosts, in that day when I publicly recognize and openly declare them to be My jewels (My special possession, My... treasure).

Malachi 3:17, AMP

I have to confess, Lord, that I don't feel at all like a precious jewel today. Help me to live in the light and the expectation of all that You have planned for me one day!

26
Prisoners

"But this is a people robbed… they are all of them snared in holes and hidden in houses of bondage… with no one to deliver them… with no one to say, Restore them!" (Isaiah 42:22, AMP). This verse seems to describe so many people I meet as a counsellor, people who have been robbed of life and joy and trapped by addiction and destructive habits. It is wonderful to watch as the Lord Himself whispers, "Restore" deep into their hearts. Jesus said He had come to bind up the broken-hearted, to proclaim freedom for the captives and release from darkness for the prisoners. He did that for me and I constantly see Him doing it for others.

> *The Spirit of the Sovereign Lord is upon me, for the Lord has anointed me… to proclaim that captives will be released and prisoners will be freed.*
>
> Isaiah 61:1, NLT

> *Please Holy Spirit, I invite You into my innermost self, asking You to show me if there are destructive habits or unhealthy thinking patterns that are holding me back from being the person You intended me to be.*

27
Where Do We Place Our Hope?

Isn't it so discouraging when we pray for years for someone we love or a difficult situation, but nothing ever seems to change. Our hope begins to fade as we wonder if God cares at all. After several bad experiences like this I've come to realize that when we place our hope in God's willingness and ability to answer our prayers *in the way we want Him to*, we are often disappointed. We need to put our hope in God's limitless intelligence and leave Him to answer our prayers at the time, and in the way, He knows is best. Our modern-day use of the word "hope" is like what we say about waiting for a bus; we hope it will come but we can't be sure. Bible hope means being *sure* of what we hope for and *certain* of what we do not see (see Hebrews 11:1).

> *This hope is a strong and trustworthy anchor for our souls.*
>
> Hebrews 6:19, NLT

> *Lord, I am letting down that "strong and trustworthy anchor" right now.*

28
Flood Tide

This morning I found this verse in my mother's old Living Bible paraphrase: "Floods of sorrow pour upon me like a thundering cataract. Yet day-by-day the Lord also pours out His steadfast love upon me" (Psalm 42:7–8). As I was wondering how "good" and "bad" could flow together, a childhood memory flagged up in my mind…

I was walking through the fields with my mother, being painfully stung by nettles. "Quick," she said, "Look for dock leaves!" After we had applied their slimy green remedy to my rash she added, "God always puts an antidote close to a poison." Now, sixty years on, I know for sure that looking for the one good thing in a nasty situation often soothes the pain like dock leaves do for stinging nettles!

Lord, I get so cross when people expect me to thank You when everything is going wrong. Yet I know that You always do hide something good among the debris! Please keep me from being too angry to recognize it.

29
The Child Inside

Sometimes it feels easy to forgive the things adults did to us in childhood because we are now adults ourselves and we understand how adults feel. So we excuse what they did out of ignorance or pressure; but excusing isn't healing – only forgiveness paves the way for healing. The hurt child inside us has been left with buried confusion, resentment, and fear and only by allowing that child to forgive from *inside* us can those strong emotions be released and healed.

Lord, help me to forgive my parents, not so much for the bad things they did, but for the good things they failed to do.

30
Forgotten Your Password?

One little word typed into my computer gives me access to so much: the entire "World Wide Web". But I have another five-letter password which opens infinitely more – JESUS. When I invoke that most powerful name in the universe it opens to me all the resources of heaven, protects me from the evils of hell and gives me the right to everlasting life! "There is no other name under heaven given to mankind by which we must be saved" (Acts 4:12).

This password is not just for me, it is yours too, so any time you sense an argument brewing, or you feel anxious or alone, just speak out your password, and you will receive all the wisdom, courage or contentment that you need.

> *At the name of Jesus every knee should bow, in heaven and on earth and under the earth.*
>
> Philippians 2:10

Lord, please help me never to forget my heavenly password!

31
Held

Sometimes, after a time of prolonged stress, a serious illness, or a major loss our spirits seem to sleep. We feel as if God is far away and the joy of His presence a thing of the past. When this happens I have often been helped by remembering that a sleeping baby is unaware of its mother's encircling arms.

> *The eternal God is your refuge, and his everlasting arms are under you.*
>
> Deuteronomy 33:27

Lord I know that You promised me that I would have Your presence with me always, but help me remember that You never promised that I would always feel Your presence.

32
Faith in His Faithfulness

Have you ever felt you were drowning in doubts about God's love and ability to care for you? "You just need more faith, dear," people say, but trying to work up enough faith to keep afloat just feels impossible. Once, I was in the middle of a serious attack of doubts, when my fourth baby became seriously ill. I felt it was my fault he wasn't recovering because I didn't have enough faith. When our vicar called I was sure he would agree!

Instead he simply said, "Don't put your trust in your faith, Jen, just focus on a faithful God." He also left a card with this verse:

> *If we are faithless, he remains faithful.*
>
> 2 Timothy 2:13

Lord, thank You for never giving up on me,
even when I feel like giving up on You!

33
Stuck in the Mud

I was woken last night by a vivid dream. In it I saw two ships, one was sailing away on an exciting adventure while the other had sunk in the mud right by the harbour wall. I felt the dream was speaking to someone who feels they have made a bad choice, which leaves them stuck in a boring situation, while other people are heading off into exciting new experiences. I think the Lord wants you to know that with Him it is never too late because He is the God of Second Chances. The ship that "foundered" can sail again one day.

> *He lifted me out of the slimy pit, out of the mud and mire; he set my feet on a rock and gave me a firm place to stand. He put a new song in my mouth, a hymn of praise to our God. Many will see and fear the Lord and put their trust in him. Blessed is the one who trusts in the Lord.*
>
> Psalm 40: 2–4

*Lord, sometimes I am so afraid of failing that
I would rather stay safely stuck in the mud
than risk sailing off on a major adventure
which might not be successful. Please give me
enough courage to become the person You
meant me to be.*

For as the heavens are high above the earth, so great are His mercy and loving-kindness toward those who reverently and worshipfully fear Him.

Psalm 103:11, AMP

34
Peace in Action

"I will be still and take hold of His peace." Someone once wrote that sentence in the front cover of my Bible. It has often reminded me it is no good just sitting and waiting for peace to pour over us. We have to deliberately take it from Him, by an act of the will.

Seek peace and pursue it.

1 Peter 3:11

"Seeking" and "pursuing" are both active, assertive words which require determination.

*Sometimes, Lord, I choose to stay distressed
and upset because I am so hurt and angry.
Help me to be willing to choose peace and set
the pain free to flow away in the wind.*

35
Scars

When we forgive someone for the wounds they have inflicted on our lives those wounds begin to heal; but the scars will always remain, identifying us with Jesus.

Scars like these always make the person who was wounded look infinitely more beautiful.

> *"Father, forgive them, for they do not know what they are doing."*
>
> Luke 23:34

Lord forgive me for "licking my own wounds" and feeling sorry for myself so often. I long for You to use me, even the most painful bits.

36
Shadows

I was talking recently with Jane, who has been struggling through depression after two major losses. "I feel I'm wandering round in a dark forest surrounded by shadows," she told me. "All I can do is keep choosing to cling to the Lord. I don't feel He is there at all, but I just have to know He is by willpower."

Opening her journal she showed me this verse, which has become her lifeline:

> *For we walk by faith, not by sight.*
>
> 2 Corinthians 5:7, AMP

Thank You, Lord, that Your light always "shines in the darkness, and the darkness can never extinguish it". (John 1:5, NLT)

37
Forgive and Forget

People often say, with a shrug, "Just forgive and forget." I believe that is totally impossible. We can never delete events from our memories but forgiving can be the determination never to allow something in the past to influence or determine the way we think or act in the future.

> Be… quick to forgive an offence. Forgive as
> quickly and completely as the Master forgave
> you. And regardless of what else you put on, wear
> love. It's your basic, all purpose garment. Never
> be without it.
>
> Colossians 3:13–14, *THE MESSAGE*

O Lord, I feel it is humanly impossible to forgive some of the things which have damaged my life. But thank You that with Your help I can even do what's humanly impossible.

38
The King's Speech

When I was a child we always listened to "The King's Speech" on Christmas afternoon. My father always finished it off for him by adding the words of King George VI's famous wartime speech in 1939, and they have always stayed in my mind.

> *"And I said to the man who stood at the gate of the year:*
> *'Give me a light that I may tread safely into the unknown.'*
> *And he replied: 'Go out into the darkness and put your hand into the Hand of God. That shall be to you better than light and safer than a known way.'"*
>
> Minnie Louise Haskins

I will lead them in paths they have not known. I will make darkness into light before them and make uneven places into a plain. These things I have determined to do, and I will not leave them forsaken.

Isaiah 42:16, AMP

Lord, I am so independent! I so often set off on projects or courses of action and then ask You to bless my plans. Please keep me always walking by Your side, in perfect step with You, hand in hand.

39
Choose Life

Recovering from a pelvic fracture took me far longer than I expected. I began feeling gloomy and sorry for myself because I was prevented from undertaking all the things I love doing, like gardening and walking in the country. The turning point came when I felt the Lord speaking to me: "Decide to take hold of life, and start enjoying the things you still have – and can still do." Then this verse popped into my mind in confirmation.

> *Arise from the depression and prostration in*
> *which circumstances have kept you – rise to a new*
> *life! Shine, be radiant with the glory of the Lord,*
> *for your light has come and the glory of the Lord*
> *has risen upon you.*
>
> Isaiah 60:1, AMP

> *Thank You for reminding me that happiness,*
> *like peace, is a choice and You want me to*
> *choose it!*

40
Snowdrops

It was early in January when I had a visit from someone who had been struggling for a long while to forgive a person who had devastated her life. I suggested she chose one of my collection of seaside stones and we carried it down to the cross at the bottom of my garden. As she laid it down as a symbolic way of letting go of her pain, we noticed a clump of early snowdrops growing by the cross. "That feels like God's promise to me of a new season, new life, and new hope," she whispered.

> *May the God of hope fill you with all joy and peace as you trust in him, so that you may overflow with hope by the power of the Holy Spirit. (Romans 15:13)*

Let us hold unswervingly to the hope we profess, for he who promised is faithful.

Hebrews 10:23

Jennifer Rees Larcombe runs "Beauty from Ashes" from her home in the heart of the Kent countryside. It is a safe place where people who are hurting come for peace, space and to receive prayer. Jennifer also runs healing days, retreats, quiet days, and conferences.

Website: www.beautyfromashes.co.uk

Contact us on: office@beautyfromashes.co.uk

www.facebook.com/beautyfromashes/JRL

Also available from Jennifer Rees Larcombe:

JENNIFER REES LARCOMBE
GOD MOMENTS
30
reflections to start or end your day

Jennifer Rees Larcombe blends observation and insight in these delightful uplifting reflections, celebrating the "God moments" that occur day by day.

These 30 succinct meditations, beautifully illustrated, each with a prayer, will make a welcome companion and a gift to treasure.

978-0-85721-693-9

www.lionhudson.com

Acknowledgments

Unless otherwise indicated, Scripture quotations are taken from the Holy Bible, New International Version Anglicised. Copyright © 1979, 1984, 2011 Biblica, formerly International Bible Society. Used by permission of Hodder & Stoughton Ltd, an Hachette UK company. All rights reserved. "NIV" is a registered trademark of Biblica. UK trademark number 1448790.

Scripture quotations marked "NKJV" taken from the New King James Version. Copyright © 1982 by Thomas Nelson, Inc. Used by permission. All right reserved.

Scripture quotations marked "The Message" taken from The Message. Copyright © by Eugene H. Peterson 1993, 1994, 1995, 1996, 2000, 2001, 2002. Used by permission of NavPress Publishing Group.

Scripture quotations marked "NLT" taken from the Holy Bible, New Living Translation, copyright © 1996, 2004, 2007 by Tyndale House Foundation. Used by permission of Tyndale House Publishers, Inc., Carol Stream, Illinois 60188. All rights reserved.

Scripture quotations marked "AMP" taken from the Amplified® Bible, Copyright © 1954, 1958, 1962, 1965, 1987 by The Lockman Foundation. Used by permission.

Scripture quotations marked "Living Bible" taken from The Holy Bible, Living Bible Edition, copyright © Tyndale House Publishers 1971. All rights reserved.

Scripture quotations marked "The Passion Translation" taken from The Passion Translation, copyright © 2015. Used by permission of BroadStreet Publishing Group, LLC, Racine, Wisconsin, USA. All rights reserved.

Extract p. 30 taken from *Candles in the Dark* by Amy Carmichael, © 1981 by The Dohnavur Fellowship. Used by permission of CLC Publications. May not be further reproduced. All rights reserved.

Extract p. 62 taken from "Great Is Thy Faithfulness" by Thomas O. Chisholm © Hope Publishing Company. Used by permission.

Picture credits:

Bill Bain: pp. 31, 59, 80, 90; Alan Bedding: pp. 77, 78; Roger Chouler: pp. 2, 4, 7, 11, 12, 14, 17, 19, 21, 29, 37, 39, 43, 48, 51, 56, 57, 59, 64, 66, 72, 73, 75, 81, 83, 85, 87, 88, 89, 94; Corbis: p. 85; Alison Hickey: p. 83; iStock: pp. 9, 60, 65, 67, 70, 71, 73, 80, 82, 83, 84, 85, 87, 88 © ollirg/iStockphoto.com; p. 13 © wwing/iStockphoto.com; p. 29 © rudisill/iStockphoto.com; p. 41 © MariaBrzostowska/iStockphoto.com; p. 53 © ngkaki/iStockphoto.com; p. 63 © Jasmin Awad/iStockphoto.com; Len Kerswill: pp. 35, 55; Andrew King: p. 43; Estelle Lobban: 11, 21, 23, 26, 33, 44, 49, 51, 61, 69, 70, 71, 73, 86, 89; Anne Rogers: pp. 15, 18, 47, 54; Nigel Ward: p. 25